#
AND THE
WORKERS

The exhibition was opened by
Her Royal Highness Princess Astrid of Norway
on 2 October 1984

ACKNOWLEDGEMENTS

We gratefully acknowledge the sponsorship of:

Newcastle Festival

Visiting Arts Unit of the British Council

Royal Norwegian Foreign Ministry

Royal Norwegian Embassy, London

Department of Education and Science

Anglo Norse Society

Marks and Spencer Plc

Sun Life Assurance Ltd

Norsk Data

Kavli Ltd

British Alcan Aluminium Ltd

Newcastle Building Society

Viking Tyres (UK) Ltd

Hovland UK Ltd

Norsk Hydro

Glamox Electric (UK) Ltd

Ulstein UK Ltd

Grorud International Sales Ltd

Britoil

Kongsberg Ltd

New England Properties plc

Borregaard Marketing Company Ltd

Bank of Scotland

Ugland UK Ltd

Nor Cargo Ltd (Newcastle and Grimsby)

ISBN 0 947940 00 6

CONTENTS

FOREWORD

In 1980 the Newcastle Polytechnic Gallery organised its first major international exhibition of 26 paintings from the Munch Museum in Oslo. It was a great success, touring to four British venues and attracting thousands of visitors as well as considerable media interest. At the time we were accused of being too ambitious; this was presumably because the Gallery was only three years' old, and for all our proven record of representing contemporary British art the Munch exhibition was indeed our first international venture.

Such an undertaking was, of course, only made possible with substantial external support and encouragement. This came from, principally, the Munch Museum which generously loaned a splendid body of work, the enlightened sponsorship of companies such as the Olsen-Bergen Line, the Visiting Arts Unit of the British Council and, significantly, the Department of Education and Science which, in granting us indemnity cover, made the exhibition viable. We were in fact the first regional gallery to be granted this facility, and in the wake of that precedent several other provincial galleries were enabled to launch exhibitions which hitherto would have been restricted to London.

Perhaps the most remarkable aspect of the 1980 exhibition, though, was the way in which it came into being independently of finance from the national and regional funding bodies, a manifestation of that spirit of enterprise expressed in Kipling's words:

"Our England is a garden, and such gardens are not made
By singing: 'Oh, how beautiful!' and sitting in the shade
While better men than we go out and start their working lives
At grubbing weeds from gravel paths with broken dinner-knives."

The same principle informs the organisation of this new exhibition 'Munch and the Workers'. Once again we are enormously indebted to Alf Böe, Director of the City of Oslo Art Collections, and Arne Eggum, Chief Curator of the Munch Museum, Oslo, for their continued support and willingness to lend so much of the

Museum's splendid collection. To his colleague Gerd Woll we are equally grateful; her catalogue introduction, at once lucid and absorbing, should do much to illuminate an aspect of Munch's oeuvre that is still too little known in Britain. To Ingebjörg Gunnarson, who has shouldered much of the administrative burden involved in setting up the exhibition, to Jan Thurmann-Moe, Head of the Restoration Department, and to the Photography Department of the Munch Museum for providing all the transparencies and photographs for this catalogue, again our many thanks.

In London, too, our Norwegian friends have been unstinting in their help. To Torbjørn Støverud, the former Cultural Attaché whose moral support was crucial in ensuring this second exhibition, and to Jan Flatla, Press and Cultural Counsellor at the Royal Norwegian Embassy whose practical advice was so valuable, our sincere gratitude.

Our sources of financial support have been no less generous; the Newcastle Festival provided the major portion of the funding and the Visiting Arts Unit of the British Council once again assisted us, while the renewal of indemnity cover by the Department of Education and Science was a vital security factor. In this context the provision of additional security facilities, involving substantial capital outlay, was both a prudent and encouraging gesture by Newcastle Polytechnic itself.

Our Norwegian friends were just as forthcoming with financial as with practical and moral support. The Royal Norwegian Foreign Ministry, the Royal Norwegian Embassy and the Anglo-Norse Society have all given us valuable grant-aid.

A special word of thanks to our commercial sponsors who are too numerous to mention here, but who broadly divide into companies based within the Tyne & Wear area and those which are British branches of Norwegian parent companies. I realise that the sponsorship of the visual arts is not always perceived as the most advantageous form of patronage, save when the exhibition has some guaranteed touristic aspect. I have been all the more delighted, therefore, with the ready enthusiasm (in some cases making exceptions to their usual policy) with which these companies have responded to our request for support of this highly serious exhibition. We greatly appreciate their help.

Finally, my ad hoc team have worked hard to make the exhibition come to fruition. They are: Stephen and Sue Bland, graphic designers; Margaret Shilling and Jude Shannon, general administration; Karen Geary, press officer and David Cheetham, translator of Gerd Woll's catalogue article. They, too, deserve the warmest praise for their contribution.

MARA-HELEN WOOD
NEWCASTLE POLYTECHNIC GALLERY

BIOGRAPHY

1863 Munch was born on the 12th December in Löten, in the county of Hedmark in Norway as the son of a strongly religious, pietist doctor. One year later the family moves to Oslo (then Christiania).

1868 Munch's mother dies at the age of 33 of tuberculosis.

1877 His 15 year old sister Sophie dies of tuberculosis.

1879/80 He studies engineering at the Technical College in Oslo which he soon gives up to become a painter. He studies art history and painting.

1882 Studio co-operative with six other artists. Christian Krogh supervises their work.

1883 Takes part in the Oslo 'Exhibition of Art and Industry' and in the autumn exhibition (annual until 1891).

1884 Contacts with the Bohème group of avant garde Norwegian (naturalist) painters and writers who involved themselves with anarchist and socialist thought, who attack handed down bourgeoise concepts of morality and speak out for sexual equality and free love.

1885 Journeys to Antwerp and Paris. (Travel grant from Frits Thaulow.) Visits to the Louvre and the Salon; particularly impressed by Manet's pictures. Starts to work on **The Sick Child, The Day After** and **Puberty.** As in the previous year he is supported from the Schäffer Legacy.'

1886 The painting **The Sick Child** together with three other pictures are shown in Oslo creating a storm of indignation in the press, and amongst the naturalist painters. Financial support from the Finne Bequest.

1889 First one-man exhibition in Oslo with 110 works. Munch takes a studio in Åsgårdstrand where he spends the summer. Receives a State scholarship. To Paris in October, enters Bonnat's art school. In November Munch's father dies. Major works this year **Spring** and **Military Band on Karl Johan Street.**

1890 ⋅ Until May in France (St. Cloud). Second State scholarship. In November he moves to Le Havre where he falls ill with rheumatic fever. Five of his pictures are burnt in the Oslo Forgyldermagasin including **The Day After** (1st version). Takes part in the autumn salon in Oslo with 10 paintings.

1890

1891 In January travels from Le Havre to Paris and Nice; returns to Norway in May. Third State scholarship; this third renewal is strongly criticised in Norwegian society. In the autumn he travels via Copenhagen to Paris and Nice. In Paris he gets to know the work of Claude Monet, Emile Bernard, Vincent van Gogh, Odilon Redon, Edgar Degas, Felix Vallotton and Toulouse-Lautrec.

1892 In March returns to Norway. (Exhibition in Oslo.) He takes part in the exhibition of the Verein Berliner Künstler (Union of Berlin Artists) which has to be closed after a week because of protests against Munch's work. Thereafter, however, they are shown in Dusseldorf, Cologne and also in Berlin. In December he travels to Berlin. He paints August Strindberg. In his diaries considerations about the social role of art appear. Major works this year **The Kiss, Puberty, Despair, Death in the Sick Room** (1st version), **Melancholy.**

1893 In Berlin Munch moves in the circle of the critics and collaborators of the newly founded magazine 'Pan': Richard Dehmel, Stanislaw Przybyszewski, Julius Meier-Graefe, Max Halbe, Arno Holz, Johannes Schlaf. Visits Dresden (exhibition), Munich (exhibition), Copenhagen (exhibition). Works on **The Frieze of Life.** This "poetry of life, love and death" is a "reaction against the spread of realism at that time". "The frieze is intended as a series of decorative pictures, which together give a picture of life. Through them all winds the curving shoreline, and beyond it the ever moving sea while under the trees, life, with all its complexities of grief and joy, carries on." (Munch)
Major works this year, **The Scream, Death and the Maiden, Madonna.**

1894 Munch continues to live in Berlin. He completes his first etchings. In September he briefly visits Stockholm (exhibition). The first lithos. In Berlin he changes his studio several times. The first publication on Munch appears (Stanislaw Przybyszewski, Willy Pastor, Frank Servaes, Julius Meier-Graefe). Exhibitions in Frankfurt, Hamburg, Dresden, Leipzig. Major works, **Angst, Ashes, The Three Stages of Woman, Vampire.**

1895 In June from Berlin via Amsterdam to Paris, then via Amsterdam to Kristiansand. Summer in Nordstrand, then – as usual – Åsgårdstrand on the Oslo fjord. September in Paris, from October Oslo (exhibition). Meier-Graefe publishes a portfolio of eight etchings by Munch. Munch's brother Andreas dies. Exhibitions in Berlin, Oslo, Bergen. Major works this year **Jealousy** and the lithos **Madonna, Vampire, The Scream.**

c1895

1896 From Berlin to Paris. Contact with the symbolists connected with Mallarmé. Programme designs for Ibsen's **Peer Gynt** and **John Gabriel Borkman** at the Théatre de L'Oeuvre, Paris. Printing of his first wood-cuts. Ten paintings in Salon des Indépendants. An article on Munch by Strindberg appears in the 'Revue Blanche'. Visits to Lysaker and Knocke in Belgium.

1897 Paris. Visit to Brussels (exhibition). Purchase of a house in Åsgårdstrand. Autumn in Oslo (exhibition with 150 works). Takes part in exhibitions in Paris and St. Petersburg. Major work, **Kiss by the Window.**

1898 In March via Copenhagen (exhibition) to Berlin, to Paris in May, to Oslo in June. First meeting with Tulla Larsen. Major work **The Red Virginia Creeper.**

Munch with Tulla Larsen. c1899

1899 Via Berlin, Paris and Nice to Florence and Rome (Raphael study scholarship) then via Paris to Nordstrand and Åsgårdstrand. In the autumn and winter convalescence in Faaberg/ Gudbrandsdalen. Takes part in the Biennale in Venice. Exhibition in Dresden. Major works this year, **The Dead Mother and the Child, The Inheritance.**

1900 To Berlin in March, then again to Florence, Rome and then to a sanatorium in Switzerland, July in Como. Munch spends the autumn in Oslo (exhibition) and the winter in Nordstrand. Major works, **Girls on the Jetty, The Dance of Life.**

1901 After summer in Åsgårdstrand in November to Berlin. Friendship with Dr. Max Linde an oculist from Lübeck who buys **Fertility** and writes a book on Munch.

1902 Winter and spring in Berlin, summer in Norway. Argument with Tulla Larsen; a gun goes off and Munch looses a joint from his finger. Late autumn in Lübeck with Dr. Linde who gives a commission for a portfolio of 14 etchings and two lithos (**From the House of Dr. Linde**). End of the year in Berlin, as always with continually changing addresses. Makes the acquaintance of a high provincial civil servant, Gustav Schiefler who starts to compile a catalogue of his prints. Exhibition of 22 paintings from **The Frieze of Life** entitled 'From the Modern Life of the Soul', in the vestibule of the Berliner Sezession in Leipzig and Oslo. Major works this year, **The Four Stages of Life, Four Girls from Åsgårdstrand.**

1903 Winter in Berlin. In March via Leipzig (exhibition) to Paris (took part in an exhibition) in April to Lübeck, in the summer Åsgårdstrand, in September to Lübeck and paints a portrait of the four sons of Linde and again to Berlin. Exhibitions in Hamburg, Oslo, Munich. Becomes acquainted with Eva Mudocci.

1904 Contracts with Bruno Cassirer in Berlin for the sale of prints, and with Commeter in

Hamburg for the sale of paintings. (In the following three years Commeter puts on several Munch exhibitions.) Membership of the Berliner Sezession. Visits Lübeck, Paris, Weimar, Drammen/Norway, Lübeck (contract work for a children's room in the Linde house). Copenhagen, Åsgårdstrand, Oslo, Berlin, Lübeck (Linde does not accept the frieze but buys pictures instead), Hamburg (portrait **Fraulein Warburg**). Exhibitions in Copenhagen, Oslo, Vienna.

1905   Berlin, Lübeck, Hamburg (portrait contract), Berlin, Åsgårdstrand, Klampenborg near Copenhagen, Chemnitz (portraits contract), Hamburg, Bad Elgersburg/Thüringia. Exhibitions in Prague (121 works), Bremen and other places. Major works this

year, portrait of Gustav Schiefler, a portrait of himself as a corpse in an operating theatre.

1906   Winter, spring and summer in Bad Kösen, Bad Ilmenau/Thüringia and Weimar. Portraits of Harry Graf Kessler, Elizabeth Förster-Nietzsche and Friedrich Nietzsche (after a photo). Meeting with Henry van de Velde. Theatre designs for Ibsen's 'Ghosts' played by Max Reinhardt's Kammerspiele at the Deutsches Theater, Berlin. End of the year again in Bad Kösen. From now on many exhibitions every year in European cities. Major work this year **Self portrait with Wine Bottle.**

Self portrait. Photo, c1906

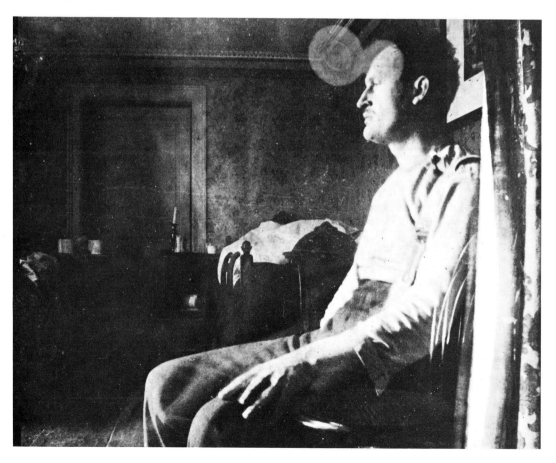

1907 Berlin (Portrait of Walter Rathenau). Scenery designs for Ibsen's 'Hedda Gabler' and decorations for a new foyer in Max Reinhardt's Kammerspiele (Reinhardt frieze). Visit to Stockholm (portrait contract), Lübeck, Warnemünde. Major works, **The Sick Child** (3rd version), **Desire, Jealousy, The Murderess** (from the cycle 'Green Room'), **Death of Marat.**

1908 From Berlin to Paris. Spring and summer in Warnemünde. The painting **Mason and Mechanic** is completed, one of the first of a series of pictures based on workmen and industry. Jens Thiis, Director of the National Gallery, Oslo, purchased several works for the museum against strong public opposition. In the autumn Munch travels via Hamburg and Stockholm to Copenhagen. Nervous breakdown. He enters a Copenhagen clinic where he is looked after for half a year. Major work, **Bathing Men.**

1909 In May Munch returns to Norway. He settles on the estate of Skrubben in Kragerø (south west of Oslo where the Oslo fjord merges into the Skagerrak). Visit to Kristiansand (southern Norway) and Bergen (exhibition). Designs for the decorations of the Oslo University Assembly Hall. In the summer a short visit to Lübeck and Berlin.

1910 Winter and spring in Kragerø. Munch buys a house in Hvitsten on the Oslo fjord. Major work, **Workers in the Snow.**

Self portrait in Warnemünde. Photo, 1908

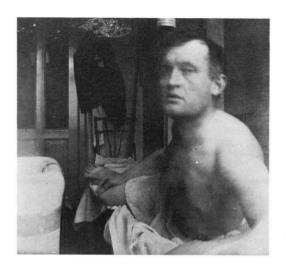

1911 The major part of the year Munch spends in Hvitsten; autumn and winter in Kragerø. He wins the competition for the University Assembly Hall but has to present new designs.

1912 In May via Copenhagen to Paris (exhibition) and Cologne (takes part in the Sonderbund exhibition with 32 paintings), he returns to Hvitsten. Major work, **Galloping Horse.**

1913 Munch rents a house in Jeløya (near Moss on the Oslo fjord). Visits to Berlin and via Frankfurt to Cologne, Paris and London. In August to Stockholm (exhibition), Hamburg, Lübeck, Copenhagen. He spends the autumn in Kragerø, Hvitsten and Jeløya. In October he is in Berlin (exhibition). Takes part in the Armory Show in New York.

1914 At the beginning of the year to Copenhagen, Frankfurt, Berlin and Paris, then via Berlin back to Kragerø, Hvitsten, Jeløya. After arguing for many years Oslo University accepts Munch's work for the Assembly Hall as a gift.

1915 Spring and summer in Hvitsten. Journeys to Trondheim and Copenhagen. Works on the pictures for the Assembly Hall. Completion of the painting **Workers Returning Home.**

1916 Munch buys Ekely, a house in Skøyen near Oslo, where he mainly resides until his death. Opening of the mural paintings in the Assembly Hall of Oslo University: "**The Frieze of Life** depicts the joys and sorrows of the individual – the pictures in the University show the great eternal forces" (Munch).

(Top) Self portrait in the sanatorium. Photo, 1908/09.
(Centre) Munch painting at 'Skrupben' (Kragerø). 1910.
(Left) Open air studio in Kragerø with decorations for the Oslo University Assembly Hall. Munch standing. c1911.

In Kragerø

1918/19 Continues working on motifs from **The Frieze of Life.** The spanish flu epidemic that is sweeping through Europe brings him down.

1920/21 Visits to Berlin (exhibitions), Paris, Wiesbaden and Frankfurt.

1922 Mural paintings for one of the dining rooms of the Freia Chocolate Factory in Oslo with motifs from the world of work. Visits to Berlin and Zürich (large retrospective). Munch buys 73 prints from German artists in order to support them.

1923 Via Berlin (exhibition) to Zürich; back via Stuttgart. Membership of the German Academy of Arts.

1924 Summer in Bergen. As in the previous year support is given to young German artists.

1925 Honorary membership of the Bavarian Academy of Visual Arts.

1926 Munch's sister Laura dies. In spring to Lübeck, Berlin, Venice, Munich (exhibition), Wiesbaden, in autumn via Copenhagen (exhibition), Berlin, Chemnitz, Leipzig, Halle, Heidelberg, Mannheim (exhibition), to Paris.

1927 In February to Berlin, in March via Munich and Rome to Florence, in April via Berlin and Dresden back to Norway. A comprehensive retrospective in the Kronprinzenpalais in Berlin and in the National Gallery in Oslo. Short visits to Berlin, Cologne and Paris.

1928 Designs for mural paintings planned for the hall of the Oslo Town Hall.

1929 The building of the winter studio in Ekely.

1930 First problems with an eye complaint.

1933 Åsgårdstrand, Hvitsten, Kragerø. Work on new designs for the Assembly Hall of the University.

1935 Major works, **The Duel (Mephistopheles I)** and **Mephistopheles II. Split Personality.**

1936 Munch gives up working on the decorations for the Oslo Town Hall because of his eye complaint.

1937 82 works of Munch's in German museums are confiscated by the Nazis. Munch supports Ernst Wilhelm Nay to enable him to stay in Norway. Large exhibitions in Stockholm and Amsterdam.

1940 Refuses any contact with the German invaders or the Norwegian collaborators. Major work self-portrait **Between Clock and Bed.**

1944 Munch dies in Ekely. He leaves all the works that are still his property: that is 1,000 paintings, 15,400 prints, 4,500 watercolours and drawings, 6 sculptures, letters and manuscripts to the City of Oslo.

"The full extent of his artistic estate was fully comprehended for the first time when, after Munch's death in 1944 in Ekely the works he had left in the deserted house were seen and put in order. The artist had lived a simple life in this house, dedicated to work. The interior had a wondrous appearance and in no way resembled a house inhabited by an ordinary mortal. Munch lived in a few sparsely furnished rooms, as if he had not really moved in and was just a passing visitor – a wandering

artist always underway . . . On the top floor of the main building, in rooms that had obviously not been lived in for many years, were massive piles of prints: thousands upon thousands of etchings, lithographs and woodcuts. Once an attempt had been made to bring them into some sort of order, but that had long since been given up.

Great piles of prints lay there covered in dust and neglected; many others were scattered over the floor. Some of the most valuable sheets had been ruined by dust, damp and sunlight. In one of these dilapidated small rooms Munch had set up his hand press. It had originally been an old fashioned kitchen, a miserable place, that had served the artist as his workshop. Everything indicated that making work easier was completely unimportant for Munch and did not help his creativity at all."
(S. Willoch, Edvard Munch's Etcher, Oslo 1950)

▲ Munch in Ekely. 1943

◄ Open air studio in Ekely. c1929

NOW IT IS THE TIME OF THE WORKERS

In February 1929 a comprehensive exhibition of Munch's graphic work opened at the National Museum in Stockholm. Munch was very preoccupied with the way that this exhibition might be received. This is apparent from some draft letters, presumably meant for Ragnar Hoppe: "I know that my way of painting has been criticised in recent years, particularly in Scandinavia. Firstly because of the large format but also because it is considered shocking to reveal the soul. The new sobriety with its treatment of detail, its smooth execution and small format has established itself everywhere . . . I can see the positive side of the case, and it may well have its uses, only I don't think it likely that this outlook will last . . . Perhaps the small format which came into fashion a hundred years ago after the victory of the bourgeoisie and which has since become the ideal format for the art dealers, will gradually disappear. It is not out of the question that art will set itself other objectives. Wall murals or similar."

"Now one should bear in mind that for the last 15 years I have been involved with large frescoes, which by their nature have taken the place of 'The Frieze of Life' . . . I regard my many small oil paintings and prints, partly, as studies . . . a necessity."

"I am sure also, that at this moment, large formats and other aspects of my art will conflict with the younger painters' conception of art. But the human element will prevail in the long run."

Then in February 1929 Edvard Munch wrote Ragnar Hoppe the following letter; "I wonder if small scale paintings will soon be pushed aside. With their large frames, they are merely a bourgeois art form designed for sitting rooms. It is an art dealer's art, a product of the French revolution, that gained strength after

◀ **Workers in the Snow**
c1913 (Cat. No. 38)
This picture for conservation reasons cannot be shown in the exhibition.

the victory of the bourgeoisie. Now it is the time of the workers. Do you not suppose that art should again become the property of everyone, and resume its rightful place on the spacious walls of public buildings?"

In a note from the end of the 1920s Munch expressed similar thoughts: "Modern architecture is composed of smooth surfaces and spaces, little pictures are no longer needed. – But the large surfaces need life and colour. The artist is given the task of covering large surfaces. Shouldn't frescoes be made again as in the Renaissance? Then art will become the property of the people – the work of art will belong to us all. The work of a painter does not need to disappear like a piece of paper inside an individual's house, where only a few people can see it. Art for large surfaces demands the total involvement of the artist, otherwise it is nothing but decoration."

These thoughts of Munch's expressed relatively late in his life, were not new. Similar considerations about art and the social function of art can also be found in his earlier writings, for the first time probably in the 1890s.

"We want something more than a simple copy of nature. Nor are we interested in painting beautiful pictures for the living room wall. We should try, even if we do not succeed, to lay the basis for an art that has something to offer. Art that takes and gives. Art that is created with the blood of the heart." "The large exhibitions are deadly for modern art – the great markets – the demand that pictures must look good on a wall – in order to decorate – not as a thing in itself not to express something."

"Who is the greatest painter in France – Meissonier? He understands best of all how to judge the wishes of the bourgeoisie. The art of our time is the art of the great Salons – the Academies – competitive art."

The Academies are great factories for painters – talent is put in and out come automated painters". "Art and money. Our age is the age of the market and the bazaar, the art of our time carries its stamp. – The great salons are nothing more than markets. The art of our time is influenced by the worst moneyed clique, namely the bourgeoisie."

In a note from the early 1930s Munch explained why he grouped many of his pictures into series or friezes: "How I became involved in mural painting and friezes . . . I have tried to resolve life and its meaning for me in my art. I also wanted to help others to see life more clearly. – I have always worked best with my paintings around me. I felt they were related in content. When I placed them together they suddenly had a resonance that alone they did not have. – Similarly they could not be effectively displayed with other pictures. That is why I assembled them into friezes."

Munch's most important and best known series of pictures is 'The Frieze of Life' on which he worked for many years. The principal motifs were developed in the early 1890s, but were later repeated in many variations. Munch looked upon the individual pictures as sketches; and hoped for a long time for the opportunity to realise 'The Frieze of Life' in an appropriate place as a monumental painting.

In the 1920s he toyed with the idea of a new large frieze dedicated to the life and industry of working men. The first evidence we have of concrete plans for this scheme, however, dates from 1921, and the designs for the mural paintings in dining rooms of the Freia Chocolate factory in Oslo. For one small dining room Munch prepared sketches for six panels. They were never executed but it was his first attempt to compose a Worker Frieze.

Later in the 1920s he made a renewed attempt in this direction on the occasion of the planned paintings for the Oslo Town Hall but again nothing came of it. For this reason the Working Man's Frieze only exists in the form of single sketches and vague designs, but the individual pictures, that were to act as the basis for the frieze belong to the major works of Munch's later period.

In Munch's early career the working people of both town and country occupied a prominent place in his art. They were part of the surroundings which the young Munch drew and painted; they became part of his pictures just as houses and trees did. In Munch's rendering of people of the lower classes one cannot find social tendencies. His art was neither programmatic nor reforming but above all things and first and foremost realistic. He depicted reality as he saw and experienced it.

A more conscious portrayal of workers can be found for the first time in pictures from the Warnemünde period, around the years 1907 and 1908. The first really monumental picture of workers 'Workers in the Snow' was painted after his return to Norway in 1909. A few years later another major new work was painted 'Workers Returning Home'.

Between the years 1910 and 1920, however, he also painted a great many large format, expressive pictures with themes from country life.

Although he did not make use of these motifs in his preparatory works for his 'Working Man's Frieze' there is no doubt that these works, too, were conceived as pictures of workers. A pointer to this can be found in exhibition catalogues from that period. The term "worker" is used often, even when it doesn't quite apply, for instance 'Agricultural Worker', 'Workers in the Garden', 'Workers in the Offshore Islands' and 'Workers Uprooting a Tree'.

Arnulf Øverland an active art critic at the time in a review in 1918 compared the pictures dealing with themes from work on the land, in this case represented by the splendid picture 'The Man in the Cabbage Field' – with 'Workers Returning Home', saying "If this picture can be seen as an idealization of people in the country, of healthy natural work, the large composition on the rear wall shows the other side of the coin, the curse of work."

He writes further on the 'Workers Returning Home'; "The emphasis on the purely pictorial, on the lines and the rhythm is so all pervading in this image of the advance of the proletariat that no one need feel threatened by any agitational motive."

Jappe Nilssen, for many years a good friend of Munch's, goes a little further in his review of the same exhibition, "Anyone with a little imagination could see the picture as an illustration of recent events in Russia".

Munch had little interest in politics. On the other hand everything suggests that he looked upon the advance of the labour movement with much sympathy. Certainly by the end of the 1920s, if not earlier, Munch saw himself as a kind of socialist. Several people who knew him or had contact with him can vouch for this. Felix Hatz who visited Munch at Ekely wrote in the catalogue for the Munch exhibition at the Malmö Art Gallery in 1975, "Munch had radical views, perhaps of a personal nature. He saw himself as a worker in this world. He was of the opinion that the hour of the workers had struck, and that it was now their turn to take over the bourgeoisie's positions. That was in 1928–29. Otherwise he had no ambitions to involve him self in politics. Any washer woman knows more about it than I do, he told me."

Workers in the Snow
1910 (Cat. No. 40)

MUNCH'S EARLY CONCERN WITH THEMES OF WORK 1880–1900

From 1875 to 1889 the Munch family lived in Grünerløkka, Christiania (the city was renamed Oslo in 1924). This part of Oslo is as densely populated today as it was at the turn of the century, characterized by large blocks of rented flats and narrow back yards. The border of this area mainly follows the river Akerselva. At the time that Munch lived there the city's major factories were near this river.

Grünerløkka was built in three phases. To start with the southern district with its little wooden houses was first built around 1860. In those days Grünerløkka was not yet part of Christiania and brick buildings were not yet compulsory. After the city was expanded the whole area became subject to new planning regulations. Even before 1875 many small brick houses were built. The last phase began about 1890. Four and five storey brick housing blocks were erected, often several blocks behind each other with narrow yards between them.

At this time the Munch family had already left Grünerløkka. While they lived in that district there was relatively little building work, apart from building extensions, which made the distance between houses shrink more and more. The Munch family moved house frequently, during the 14 years they spent in Grünerløkka they had 5 different addresses – always new houses.

Despite the brick houses of the 60s and 70s the district had a predominantly rural character. The people living in Grünerløkka were for the most part craftsmen, minor white collar employees and workers with regular jobs.

The reason why the Munch family in 1875 moved from a spacious flat in the city centre to a much more restricted flat in a new suburb like Grünerløkka is not known. The father had a secure income as a regimental physician. So the reasons cannot have really been financial. Grünerløkka didn't exactly have the best reputation in Christiania's polite society, but it

was in no way a poor quarter. Perhaps it was the new houses of Grünerløkka that were attractive, with their running water in the kitchen and a wc on the landing – advantages which the old houses in the west of the city did not have to offer. In addition the rural character of the area may have played a role for the Munch family, as tuberculosis, pneumonia and bronchitis were a daily threat in those days.

The children of the family do not appear to have played much outside the houses with other children from the neighbourhood. Fear of sickness and class differences probably meant that they mostly stayed amongst themselves. They seem to have spent many hours of their lives in the house. In such situations, the window plays a very important role. It isn't surprising therefore that it became a much used element in Edvard Munch's art. The window became the opening to everything that was happening outside, in which he couldn't take part.

Amongst the earliest works of his youth sketches from his closest environment predominate; objects and people in the house; the view through the window. As he gradually became more sure of himself, he took his drawing equipment outside. However, in doing so he concentrated totally on the surroundings and people from the immediate neighbourhood. In November 1880 he decided to become a painter and left the technical college which he had attended for barely a year. During this time he was continually out and about with his drawing utensils, either alone or with other artists who he met in the drawing school or elsewhere. From the beginning of the 1880s there are a great number of sketches, drawings and small oil paintings depicting Christiania and its surrounding areas. Landscapes dominate, but there are also people in these pictures – tired women and men wandering along roads.

In the mid 1880s Munch came in contact with the "Christiania-Bohème" in which the painter

◀ **Woman at a Loom.** 1882 (Cat. No. 4)

Christian Krohg and the author Hans Jäeger set the tone. Although Munch always remained on the periphery of this circle, it cannot be denied that their radical opinions on art and politics had an extremely strong influence on him.

Munch's pictures from the end of the 1880s are clearly influenced by Krohg's Naturalism and in his diaries he tries in the style of Jäeger, "to describe his life".

The regimental physician Christian Munch always made a point of taking his family to the countryside for the summer. This was still unusual for most people, firstly because they only had a few free days and also because they had enough trouble simply earning sufficient money for daily life. It was only among the more well-to-do citizens that it had become the custom to own or rent a summer house.

The Munch family couldn't afford to own a place for the summer, with the help of relatives and acquaintances they managed neverthe-less to go to the countryside.

When Edvard was born the Munchs lived on a farm in Löten, Hedmark. When he was barely a year old they moved away, but the contact with the people on the farm remained. The 19 year old artist spent the summer of 1882 in familiar places in Hedmark where he often drew people at work and at rest.

Munch had scholarships from the Norwegian government for the years 1889 to 1891 – (Kr 1500 for the first two years and Kr 1000 for the third year) which allowed him to travel and study art abroad. During these three years he spent most of his time in France.

Around the 1st of October 1889 he travelled to Paris where he studied painting under Bonnat, together with some other young Norwegian artists. He is said to have worked diligently at Bonnat's but the decisive influence upon him came from the impressions and stimulation he found in the museums and galleries.

At the turn of the year 1889/90 he moved out of Paris to St. Cloud. He lived there relatively isolated from the Scandinavian artists' colony apart, that is, from the Danish poet Emanuel Goldstein his closest friend. He mixed a great deal with the locals and wrote to his aunt Karen "I associate only with French workers and other citizens of St. Cloud – I talk with them as well as I can and in doing so learn a little French. All the lower class people here are tremendously friendly." 15.1.1890.

At that time he painted several pictures of restaurants and bars which were clearly influenced by the recently published "Les Types de Paris" by Raffaelli.

Sketches of Ordinary People
c1881 (Cat. Nos. 1, 2)

Girl Standing with a Rake.
1882 (Cat. No. 3)

Haymaking.
1883 (Cat. No. 5)

Morning in Grünerløkka.
1885 (Cat. No. 7)

On the back is a pencil drawing of a standing worker. For work clothes undyed cotton was used, because it was cheap. Munch, in the later 1880s, dealt with the phenomenon of light clothing seen in early morning light or the dying light of the evening. In one of his diaries he tells how he and two friends travelled home late one night after a party, "Outside I could make out the light trousers of a worker on his way to work".

**Workers in the light of a gas
lantern.**
c1885 (Cat. No. 8)

From Tiergarten, Berlin
1896 (Cat. No. 10)

FISHERMEN, FARMERS, BEGGARS AND WORKERS IN GERMANY AND NORWAY 1900–1910

In 1892 Munch was invited to exhibit in Berlin. Even though the exhibition ended in a scandal it attracted the attention of several German art dealers who offered to arrange exhibitions elsewhere. This established Munch's fame at an international level. Until 1909 he spent most of his time abroad. Apart from a few lengthier stays in Paris he spent most of the time in Germany preferably in Berlin where he joined a group of artists. It didn't differ greatly from those at home. In some cases they were the same people he had known in Scandinavia. The ever increasing number of exhibitions and commissions for portraits took him all over Germany.

There are very few pictures from the 1890s in which Munch painted workers. At this time he created his most important pictures for the 'Frieze of Life', with its major themes of love, sickness and death. He called them "Pictures from the Modern Life of the Soul".

The first years of this century were for Munch, very hectic but productive years of work. Everyday experiences and everyday people start to reappear in his paintings and etchings around that time.

He spent the summer of 1907 and 1908 in Warnemünde, a small fishing town on the Baltic not far from Rostock and described the town as a "German Åsgårdstrand" in his letters to his family. Here he painted several pictures in which working people take a central place. Perhaps the best known is 'Mason and Mechanic' which is often described as his first picture of working men. 'Worker and Child' has meanwhile come to be considered equally significant.

◀ **Old Skipper** 1899 (Cat. No. 11)   **Standing Worker** 1902 (Cat. No. 12)

The Fisherman and his Daughter
1902 (Cat. No. 13)

Portrait of a Man (Worker)
1903 (Cat. No. 16)

The Cripple
After 1910 (Cat. No. 27)

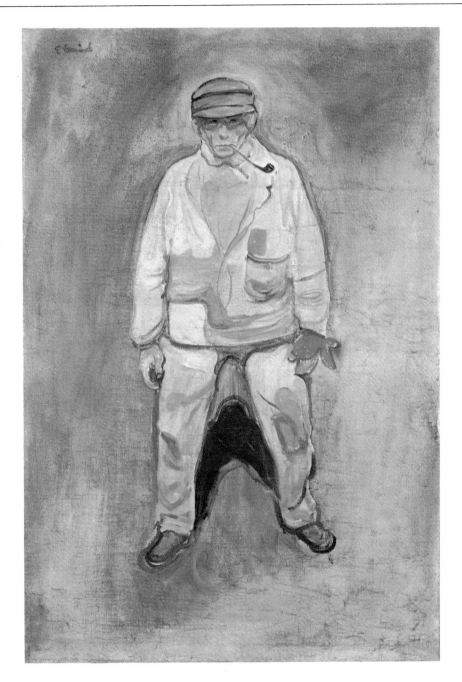

Fisherman on a Green Meadow
c1902 (Cat. No. 14)

This picture is known by several titles, most often as 'Fisherman'. It was exhibited in 1912 in several German cities with the title 'Worker in the Meadow'. Munch himself describes it in letters around that time as 'Worker with a red cloth in his hand'.

Cleaning Women on the Stairs
c1906 (Cat. No. 18)

Old Man in Warnëmunde
1907 (Cat. No. 19)

Mason and Mechanic
1908 (Cat. No. 20)

Worker and Child
1908 (Cat. No. 22)

PEOPLE AND SURROUNDINGS IN KRAGERØ AROUND 1910

After many restless years with a high consumption of alcohol Munch had a breakdown in 1908 and had himself committed to Dr. Daniel Jacobson's clinic in Copenhagen. After a stay of several months he travelled to Norway in April 1909. Near Kragerø he discovered the estate at Skrubben which he immediately rented. After several trips to Norway and abroad in the summer, he settled down in Skrubben in autumn 1909 and began serious work on the Oslo University Assembly Hall mural competition. The time on Skrubben was a very productive period for Munch. He was not short of new ideas and plans and worked with breathtaking speed on his monumental major works.

In the Kragerø period the surroundings appear to have played an important role for Munch, and everything suggests that he felt very happy there. Kragerø had once been an important port. It was the custom that all boys spent a few years at sea before settling down in their hometown. This had probably contributed to the people there having a wider horizon than would be usual in small isolated towns. Munch felt that this was very positive. He reports in a note "At Kragerø and along the coast there is another sort of man – one finds a livelier, more alert way of thinking – more phosphorus in the brain – does that come from the fish? I think it goes back to the distant past when they all had contact with Europe and the world."

Two old seamen, Børre Eriksen and Ellef Larsen, were part of his household on Skrubben; they worked as odd-job men and served as models. Two splendid women were at Skrubben as well. They looked after the household, sewing linen and dealing with much else. Apart from them the master decorator (and amateur artist) Lars Fjeld helped with the large designs for the Assembly Hall murals.

Seamen in the Snow
1910 (Cat. No. 29)
This picture was also shown under other titles: 'Seamen going over the Mountains' (Blomqvist 1918), 'Workers in the Snow' (National Gallery, Oslo, 1927).

Scrapping a Ship (Kragerø). 1911 (Cat. No. 33)

**Men in the Snow in Light and
Dark Clothes**
c1911 (Cat. No. 32)

(Top) **Fisherman on a Snow Covered Coast**
1910/11 (Cat. No. 31)

Man with a Sledge
c1912 (Cat. No. 34)

WORKERS IN THE SNOW 1909–1913

In June 1909 Munch and his cousin Ludrig Orning Ravensberg made a sea voyage from Kragerø to Bergen where there was an exhibition of Munch's work; they stayed for a few days. For their return journey they chose a route over the mountains. The route can be easily reconstructed through a sketchbook in which many drawings have place names. It is clear, for example, that most of the drawings in this sketchbook were created in the first two weeks of July 1909.

Immediately before a sketch with the title 'Tinnsjø' we find two sketches which strongly resemble the later painting 'Workers in the Snow'. It is to be presumed, therefore, that this motif is based on the drawings in the sketch-book made on that journey. Presumably Munch on his way through the Telemark met a group of workers who may have been laying a road or a railway track. On a third sketch in the same book between well known Kragerø motifs, to the right of the workers can be seen the suggestion of a path or similar. It is no longer possible to decide if this sketch was made at the same time as the two others or if it came later.

Heavy industry established itself in the Tele-mark during those years. Wandering casual labourers or "slusker" (navvies) as the Norwegians liked to call them, have stamped their mark on the character of the valleys around Tinnsjø. Building work in Notodden was already completed in 1909 but in Vestfjordtal towards Rjukan the work was still in full swing.

Assuming the original motif can be traced back to those sketches an interesting development can be seen. Presumably inspired by models in

◀ **Men Clearing Snow**
1913/14 (Cat. No. 39)
This motif is closely related to the theme of 'Workers in Snow'. A better version in the National Galerie, Berlin, was lost during the Second World War.

Kragerø Munch continued to work on these motifs through autumn and winter of 1909–10. A sketch showing a central figure naked with a pick over his shoulder and in the same pose as the workers, could be seen as an intermediate stage of this development. Similarly many sketches of the central figure of 'Workers in the Snow' exist, for which there must have been a model. In these sketches it is possible to discern his bearing and form becoming gradually more and more monumental.

We do not quite know what caused Munch to begin monumental portrayals of workers. But it is not surprising that he chose casual labourers such as these "navvies" as representatives of that level of society. Their predecessors – such as miners and stone breakers had already found a place in art history through Courbet and van Gogh. Apart from that, Dalou, Rodin and Meunier had already attempted to illustrate their significance, at the turn of the century, through designs for workers' memorials.

It is also relevant that casual labourers in the years around 1910 were members of a militant labour movement in Norway and therefore presented an ideal subject for the honouring of workers.

There are a variety of hints to suggest that Munch felt close to these rootless, wandering men. Much later in his life – probably when he picked up the motif again for the mural painting of the Oslo Town Hall – Munch wrote about the central figure of the picture; "As long as I have been painting in this country I have had to fight for every foot of ground for my art with clenched fists – In my big worker picture I have also painted as the central figure a man with his fists clenched."

Another drawing from 1909/10 makes it clearer that Munch began to identify with the workers at that time or rather, began to realise that the workers and he were involved in the same struggle against the same enemy, the bourgeoisie.

In three very similar sketches from two sketch pads we can see a powerful, naked arm raised threateningly in the air. The fist is clenching a short shafted hammer. Behind the arm we can see a group of people and behind them the gable end of a house stands out against the skyline. On one of these sketches Munch has written Christiania on the gable end so that we know in which city we are. The drawing resembles a caricature from the immediately preceeding years; on the extreme right the characteristic figure of Christian Krohg can be seen. Munch most probably wanted to say that the labour movement was threatening Christiania and also the now hated Bohème group with annihilation. He himself had felt rejected and scorned by the conservative citizens of Christiania and for many years had avoided the city of his childhood.

Workers with Picks and Shovels
1909/10 (Cat. No. 36)

Workers in the Snow
1909/10 (Cat. No. 37)

This picture is possibly the earliest version of the motif. Presumably it was exhibited in March 1910 in the Diorama restaurant in Christiania together with the picture 'The Beggar'.

AGRICULTURAL AND FORESTRY WORK, FERTILITY MOTIFS 1910–1916

Munch depicted a variety of scenes from his life on the various farms he rented or owned in Kragerø, Hvitsten, Jeløy and Ekely. A certain degree of agricultural activities were pursued on these farms even if they were limited mainly to gardening. Munch laid great value on keeping a horse though it was used purely as a model and not for practical work. It was not just work on the land that inspired him, but forestry work in the woodlands near his country seat also served as the basis for several large pictures.

In his pictures of agricultural and forestry work we often find more than a reproduction of everyday motifs of work. Munch was particularly interested in 'creativity', which he often revealed in his art. Whether a house was being built, or seed sown or a harvest gathered in, all the pictures depicted something new being produced. In his paintings on agricultural themes the workers are picking the fruit of their own labours. Munch's homage to fertility was just as much a homage to the work of mankind. This is clearly expressed in his painting 'Fertility' in which we see a middle-aged man and woman under a tree, both marked by the toil of life.

Fertility
c1902 (Cat. No. 41)

Life (right section)
c1910 (Cat. No. 43)

◀ **Woodcutter** 1913 (Cat. No. 46)

Harvesting Machine
c1916 (Cat. No. 49)

Man Digging
1915(?) (Cat. No. 48)

WORKERS RETURNING HOME 1913–1920

Although Munch painted his large picture of workers on their way home from the factory as late as 1913 when he was in Moss on the Oslo fjord, the scene must have been in his mind for most of his life. He had already depicted workers on their way to and from work in sketches in the 1880s it had been a familiar scene for him ever since his youth in Grünerløkka. One of the largest factories there, a sail cloth factory, had been quite near to the Munch house and Edvard had certainly experienced daily, the workers hurrying home.

In the archives of the Folk Museum for "Work" there is a vivid report from one of the people who had been there: "The factory shut at 6 o'clock – then it was like the 17th May (National holiday) on Karl Johan, the main street. Between 800 and 900 people worked here then. Some went straight along the Seilduksgata (Sail Cloth Street) others down the Fossveien and over to Olaf-Ryes square, from where they streamed out in various directions. The area outside the main gate of this was always black with people when they poured out in the evening to get home."

In 1930 Munch's sister Inger photographed the workers leaving the Sail cloth factory on a Saturday. The motif is essentially no different from the scene her brother reproduced in his paintings of workers leaving other factories.

As was the case with his other main works Munch painted two versions of 'Workers Returning Home'. One is hanging in the Statens Museum in Copenhagen and the other belongs to the Munch Museum. The pictures were shown in most large Munch exhibitions after 1915 and in the first years attracted considerable critical attention. After an exhibition in Liljevalchs Konsthall in 1917 Ragnar Hoppe wrote in Ord och Bild (Word and Picture): "This delineation of worn out people wandering home, marked by many long hours in the factory, is a masterly observation in both expression and movement in a way that Munch could hardly have achieved earlier. The expressions, the way they are moving out like a never ending stream. The terrible desolation of a sunless back street where they drag themselves through the cold blue shadows of the houses. This movement, which has nothing in common with impressionistic, photographic snaps, is new and modern and alive with its own energy. All this is more than admirable. Munch's best works have a suggestive effect that prompts strong emotions, firstly through his themes and secondly through completely abstract, aesthetic moments."

"Quite apart from the subject, the observer, in looking at a painting like the one described above, is drawn into the creative process. The power that raged in the artist's breast as he set to work fills us all."

◄ **Workers Returning Home**
1913/15 (Cat. No. 53)
A slightly smaller version of this picture is in the Statens Museum, Copenhagen. The motif presumably originates from Moss where Munch had rented a large estate in 1913. When first exhibited this picture was entitled 'Workers'.

Workers Returning Home
c1913 (Cat. No. 52)

**Workers Returning Home and a
Man with a Top Hat**
1916 (Cat. No. 54)

Workers on the Road
After 1916 (Cat. No. 55)

Grenadier-strasse, Berlin
1919/20 (Cat. No. 57)

CITY MOTIFS, BUILDING WORK, CONSTRUCTION OF THE STUDIO 1920s

In Ekely, Munch lived to some extent like an eccentric recluse. Nevertheless, he was interested in the life and activities of the streets and construction sites. He kept the sketches as material for future pictures.

In 1946 in an article entitled "Edvard Munch's Style – Designs for an Investigation", Axel L. Romdahl described the situation, "I remember how when we were both hanging his pictures for the Jubilee Exhibition in Göteborg Edvard Munch suddenly felt like drawing some workers who were struggling with a large stone slab on a building on Göta square. With a few lines he invented a perfect, handsome composition. He was thinking of using this study in mural paintings for the Oslo Town Hall which he hoped one day to be able to carry out, but the sketch was never used. I saw it again at Munch's house and would have liked to have it for our Museum but I couldn't even ask him to reserve it as I knew that all the work Munch heaped up around himself he wouldn't give away at any price as he needed it all, considering it necessary work material and a source of inspiration. 'Street Workers in Snow', from 1920, gives an idea of the splendid composition of the drawing of which I am thinking. The picture is evidence for the spontaneous monumentality of the later Munch."

After all those years in which Munch had managed with his open air studio, with paintings hanging outside in summer and winter, he decided at the end of the 1920s to build an indoor studio at Ekely. The building was designed by an old friend, the architect Henrick Bull, and built in 1929. Thus Munch gained urgently needed work and storage space. He appears not to have missed any opportunity to draw and paint the building workers from close by. Around this time he also occupied himself with plans for decorations for the proposed new Town Hall in Oslo and as he planned to depict its construction it is reasonable to conjecture that he conceived this aspect of that project when he was drawing the building of his own winter studio.

◀ **Street Workers**
1920 (Cat. No. 74)
A painted version is owned by a private collector. Along with 'Workers in the Snow' and 'Men clearing Snow' this is the third motif Munch planned to use in his large composition for the decoration of the Oslo Town Hall.

Workers
1920s (Cat. Nos. 77, 78, 80)

Workers in the Cellar
1918 or earlier (Cat. No. 70)

Horse and Cart in the Street
c1920 (Cat. No. 71)

Workers Leaving the Building Site
c1920 (Cat. No. 81)

Building Work
c1920 (Cat. No. 84)

Worker and Horse
1920s (Cat. No. 86)

Building Workers
1920s (Cat. No. 91)

Building Workers under the Roof
1920s (Cat. No. 92)

Building Work
1929(?) (Cat. No. 99)

Horses in the Street
(Cat. No. 72)

Fire
1920/22 (Cat. No. 75)

Building Work
1920s (Cat. No. 87)

Building Work
1920s (Cat. No. 88)

Building Work
1929(?) (Cat. No. 98)

On the back is another drawing
of building work in red pencil.

Building Work
c1929 (Cat. No. 101)

Building of the Winter Studio
1929 (Cat. No. 102)

This painting was reproduced in the Arbeiderbladet newspaper in December 1929, with the following text: "A study of Munch's new studio made during the building work. The design for a possible Munch Hall in the future Oslo Town Hall?" In an exhibition in 1938 in Oslo this picture is shown as 'Workers'.

THE FREIA PROJECT
DESIGNS FOR MURALS IN THE DINING
ROOMS OF A CHOCOLATE FACTORY 1921

The Freia Chocolate Factory in Rodeløkka, Oslo, had under the direction of Johan Throne Holst quickly developed into an important enterprise. At the beginning of the 1920s it had virtually come to be regarded as a model factory. In order to establish this with the world at large Throne Holst decided to have the factory decorated with works of art. He started at the beginning of 1921 by opening negotiations with Munch about decorations for the dining rooms. In 1921 the Freia had three dining rooms on its top floor. It is not clear to what extent the factory wanted artistic decoration. In the Munch Museum there are designs for two rooms, but it was only the designs for the largest room that were realised. The sketches are, according to the commission, on a scale of 1:10. They are mounted on cardboard on which the original layout of the wall is drawn. From the sketches it is quite easy to imagine how the unrealised paintings would have looked.

With these designs on cardboard Munch attempted to create a new frieze, a working man's frieze made up of six panels with themes from the life of the workers outside the factory.

The most important picture in this frieze is 'The Workers Leaving the Factory'. It would have been the largest panel in the frieze if it had been realised. The motif and composition are connected with 'Workers Returning Home from Eureka' created by Munch one year earlier. In two further panels we can follow the workers on their way home through the city. In 'The Mechanic Meets his Daughter' picture we are still in the immediate vicinity of the factory. The motif is the same as the 'Worker and Child' picture from Warnemünde except that the open sea of Warnemünde has been replaced with a long, desolate factory wall.

The Trinity church does not relate specifically to the workers but is a familiar sight and point of orientation for the workers wandering through Oslo. The next two panels show the workers during their leisure time – Saturday evening on a bench in the little park of Studenterlunden and Sunday, a trip to the woods in Grefsenåsen. Both these pictures contain older motifs that have nothing to do with the workers theme.

It is difficult to place the last picture of the series 'A Chat by the Fence' within the Working Man's Frieze, and it was left out in his later attempts to realise the Frieze. But in the small canteen-room at Freia, it might have offered an acceptable link to the decoration of the large dining room for which he revived many of the old Åsgårdstrand motifs of the 'Frieze of Life' pictures.

After the dining room had been moved to the ground floor and the pictures fixed onto the new walls Munch wrote, "The Freia pictures have now been put up in the large dining room on the ground floor where they are effective. The employees and workers of Freia are highly enthusiastic, and even the little chocolate girls who eat there understand the pictures more and more. The 'Frieze of Life' has been transferred to another location. It deals with the life of a fisherman in a coastal town untroubled by tourists."

◀ **In Studenterlunden**
1921 (Cat. No. 63)
This carries the title 'I Studenterlunden' (Cat. No. 62 is glued onto the same sheet of cardboard).

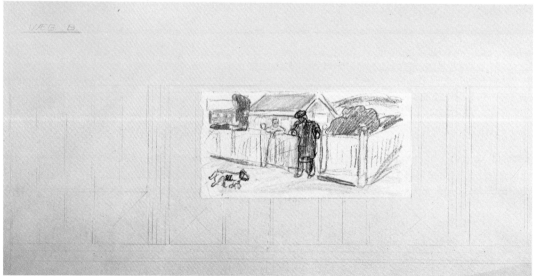

Workers Leaving the Factory
1921 (Cat. No. 59)
Glued on to cardboard and marked 'Sal 1 Vaeg D' (Hall 1 Wall D). It carries the title, 'Arbeiderne strömmer ut av fabrikken'.

A Chat by the Fence
(Cat. No. 64)
Glued to cardboard, marked 'Sal 1 Vaeg B' (Hall 1 Wall B). It carries the title, 'En passiar ved stakittet'. The designs for the decorations that were carried out are glued to the same type of cardboard,

marked 'Sal II' and with alphabetical indications for the various walls. The designs are carried out fairly precisely at a ratio of 1:10 as the contract stipulated. One can presume that this also applied to the plan for the designs for Hall 1.

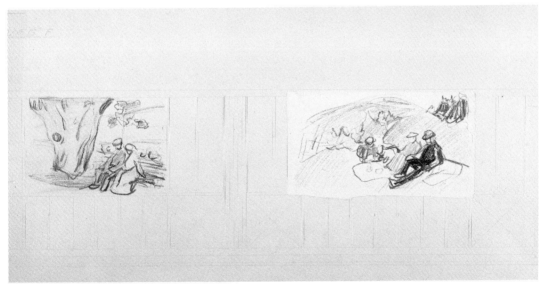

Mechanic meets his Daughter
1921 (Cat. No. 60)

Trinity Church
1921 (Cat. No. 61)

Glued on to cardboard and marked 'Sal 1 Vaeg C' (Hall 1 Wall C) Cat. No. 61 is drawn on the same sheet of cardboard. It carries the title, 'Mekanikeren mötor sin datter'. The motif is the same as the picture 'Worker and Child' of 1908.

Stroll to Grefsenåsen
1921 (Cat. No. 62)
Glued to cardboard and marked 'Sal 1 Vaeg F' (Hall 1 Wall F). It carries the title, 'Tur til Grefsenåsen'.

In Studenterlunden
1921 (Cat. No. 63)

THE TOWN HALL PROJECT
DESIGNS FOR THE MURAL PAINTINGS
IN THE OSLO TOWN HALL 1927–1933

The plan to build a new Town Hall for Christiania was already a hundred years old when in 1915 Hieronymus Heyerdahl organised a collection for it. The plan was to build the new town hall in the district of Pipervika. Despite the war raging in the rest of Europe the campaign was an overwhelming success. In 1918 an architectural competition was set for its design and it was won by Magnus Poulson and Arnstein Arneberg. Nevertheless, many years passed before building work could begin. In the meantime the architects continued to produce new and improved designs.

It was obvious that the capital needed a sufficiently representative building, and it was therefore not surprising that the idea arose that Munch should decorate it. The idea was launched in 1927 by Haldis Stenhamar in an interview in the Dagbladet newspaper. "Later our conversation turned to the Town Hall, and I ask as an ordinary citizen of this country if it would not be a reasonable idea to plan the inclusion of the 'Frieze of Life' in the great hall of the new Oslo Town Hall. It must be possible to plan and discuss this now with the architects while detailed drawings are still being worked on. The years are drifting by and God knows when the Town Hall will be ready. At present Munch is still with us."

The plan gained widespread support, but Munch did not seem to have been particularly enthusiastic about using the 'Frieze of Life' in such a context. However, he could very well consider decorating the City Hall with a frieze on the subject of working life in Oslo. In an interview in 1928, Munch gave a good description of the way he conceived such a decoration:

"I am greatly interested in the plans to make a frieze on the subject of working life in Oslo," Munch said . . .

"Is this an idea you have been working on for a

Building of the Town Hall c1929 (Cat. No. 111)

long time, the idea of portraying the life of the city in pictures?"

"They're not actually pictures of the city except in that I've been very much interested in painting workers at their work, masons working on a new building, men digging up the street, and so forth. When I was going to do the decorations out at Freia, I did various sketches of workers on their way home from the factory and similar subjects. In a way, I have seen all these experiments as part of a whole, but I'm still far from clear about how much I would include if I came to work them together. Perhaps I could also work in some of the things I have been involved with earlier – timber-felling, the black and the

◀ **Horse on a Building Site** 1920s (Cat. No. 105)

white horse drawing the load of timber, etcetera. Possibly it would be best just to keep to the city, and various streets and buildings, the harbour and other things would be included, of course, even if the figures were the essential element . . ."

"It might be an idea to paint the whole thing covered in snow, it would be a way of getting a sort of pervading unity. A picture of snow at an exhibition eclipses just about all the others, but if everything else was painted in white and yellow as a background to the strong colours of the figures . . ."

As the principal picture of the decorations. Munch seems to have kept two alternatives in mind:
1. the City Hall under construction, with a throng of construction workers on the job; and
2. a big composition based on the 'Workers in Snow' motive.

He worked on both these ideas side by side, and it is very difficult to establish any tenable chronology for the individual sketches or ideas.

Later on, the plans expand in both content and scope – Munch brings in Oslo's history and tries at the same time to realize the 'Worker Frieze' as he had intended it for the dining room at Freia in 1921.

But he was never to receive any final commission for the decoration, and when the foundation stone of the City Hall was at last laid in 1931, Munch was almost seventy years old and suffering from an eye complaint which made it impossible for him to paint.

GERD WOLL
CURATOR,
MUNCH MUSEUM, OSLO

Building of the Town Hall
c1929 (Cat. No. 112)

**The Town Hall Under
Construction**
1929 or earlier (Cat. No. 106)

Workers in the Snow
c1930/33 (Cat. No. 116)

Building of the Town Hall
c1929 (Cat. No. 108)

Building of the Town Hall
c1929 (Cat. No. 109)

Building of the Town Hall
c1929 (Cat. No. 110)

Building of the Town Hall
c1929 (Cat. No. 113)

Workers in the Snow
1929 (Cat. No. 114)

Following preparatory discussions for the Munch exhibition at Blomqvist this picture was published in the Arbeiderbladet newspaper. The photograph was accompanied by the following text: "The large exhibition of Munch's graphic work which was shown at the National Gallery in Stockholm can be seen on Friday at Blomqvist's. It is the largest exhibition of his graphic work that Munch has shown so far. As well as earlier, known works, completely new and very interesting items can be seen. We are referring to designs and sketches for the major work that has occupied our great artist for many years. A cycle of pictures on working life in the city. Edvard Munch has chosen this motif for the decoration of our future Town Hall. Here we show a detailed study from the major work, a sketch on the theme of 'building'."

Workers in the Snow
c1930 (Cat. No. 115)

CATALOGUE

Early Concerns with Work as a Theme 1880–1900

1. Sketches of Ordinary People.
c1881, chinese ink, 33.5 × 50cm.
OkkT1270/St.11.

2. Sketches of Ordinary People.
c1881, pencil, 15 × 24.5cm.
Okk T85/St.12.

3. Girl Standing with a Rake.
1882, pencil, 31.3 × 23.8cm.
OkkT717/St.29.

4. Woman at a Loom.
1882, pencil, 32.6 × 23.3cm.
OKKT497/St.30.

5. Haymaking.
1883, pencil, 24.6 × 34cm.
Okk T2360/St.31.

6. From the Life of a Rag
Collector.
c1884, ink, 18.8 × 25cm.
Okk T87/St.16.

7. Morning in Grünerløkka.
1885, pencil, 31.2 × 42.2cm.
Okk T445/St.19.

8. Workers in the Light of a Gas
Lantern.
c1885, pen and ink, 36.1 × 23.7cm.
Okk T111/St.20.

9. Street Scene in Christiania.
Before 1889, pen and ink, 21.4 ×
28cm.
Okk T1265/St.21.

9. ▲

10. From Tiergarten, Berlin.
1896, etching, 11.9 × 15.2cm.
Sch.54/Okk G/r42-27/St.44.

Fishermen, Farmers, Beggars and Workers in Germany and Norway 1900–1910

11. Old Skipper.
1899, woodcut, 44.1 × 35.7cm.
Sch.124/RES B356/St.62.

12. Standing Worker.
1902, etching, 43 × 11cm.
Sch.146/OkkG/r56-5/St.55.

13. The Fisherman and his
Daughter.
1902, etching, 47.5 × 61.3cm.
Sch.147/Okk G/r57- 7/ St.56.

14. Fisherman on a Green
Meadow.
c1902, oil/canvas, 80 × 61cm.
Okk M474/St.64.

15. ▲

15. Heads of Two Men (Workers).
1903, etching, 46.8 × 61.5cm.
Sch.197/Okk G/r92-5/St.60.

16. Portrait of a Man (Worker).
1903, etching, 49.6 × 32.3cm.
Sch.201/OkkG/r96-6/St.61.

17. Cleaning Women on the
Landing.
1906, gouache and coloured
crayon, 71.6 × 47.5cm.
Okk T534/St.51.

18. Cleaning Women on the
Stairs.
c1906, gouache, charcoal,
coloured crayon, 71 × 80cm.
Okk M1069/St.49.

19. Old Man in Warnëmunde.
1907, oil/canvas, 110 × 85cm.
Okk M491/St.67.

20. Mason and Mechanic.
1908, oil/canvas, 90 × 69.5cm.
Okk M574/St.68.

21. The Drowned Boy.
1908, oil/canvas, 85 × 130cm.
Okk M559/St.69.

21.▲

22. Worker and Child.
1908, oil/canvas, 76 × 90cm.
Okk M563/St.70.

23. Worker and Child.
1908, charcoal, 55.7 × 79.8cm.
Okk T1853/St.71.

24. The Rag Collector.
1908/09, etching, 60 × 44cm.
Sch. 131/Okk G/r 131.

25. The Rag Collector.
1908/09, ink, 17.8 × 22.1cm.
Okk T1649.

26. The Beggar.
1909/10, oil/canvas, 215 × 140cm.
Okk M715.

27. The Cripple.
After 1910, coloured pencil, 50.6 ×
35.4cm.
Okk T1656.

28. The Cripple.
After 1910, ink, 13.8 × 22.5cm.
Okk T1648.

People and Surroundings in Kragerø around 1910

29. Seamen in the Snow.
1910, oil/canvas, 95 × 76cm.
Okk M493/St.94.

30. Workers in the Snow.
c1910, oil/canvas, 93 × 94.5cm.
Okk M286/St.89.

31. Fishermen on a Snow
Covered Coast.
1910/11, oil/canvas, 103.5 ×
128cm.
Okk M425/St.87.

32. Men in the Snow in Light and
Dark Clothes.
c1911, oil/canvas, 59 × 52cm.
Okk M926/St.90.

33. Scrapping a Ship
1911, oil/canvas, 110 × 110cm.
Okk M439/St.95.

34. Man with a Sledge.
c1912, oil/canvas, 65 × 115.5cm.
Okk M761/St.91.

35. Man with a Sledge.
c1912, oil/canvas, 77 × 81cm.
Okk M472/St.92.

Workers in the Snow
1909–1913

36. Workers with Picks and
Shovels.
1909/10, charcoal, 62.7 × 47.8cm.
Okk T1852/St.102.

37. Workers in the Snow.
1909/10, oil/canvas, 210 × 135cm.
Okk M889/St.122.

38. Workers in the Snow.
c1913, oil/canvas, 163 × 200cm.
Large photograph.

39. Men Clearing Snow.
1913/14, oil/canvas, 191.5 × 129cm.
Okk 902/St.126.

40. Workers in the Snow.
1910, bronze, 70 × 56.5 × 45cm.
Okk S1/St.125.

Land and Forestry Work,
Fertility Motifs, 1910–1916

41. Fertility.
c1902, oil/canvas, 128 × 152cm.
Okk M280/St.144.

42. Life (left section).
c1910, oil/canvas, 134.5 × 147cm.
Okk M728/St.145.

43. Life (right section).
c1910, oil/canvas, 136 × 135.5cm.
Okk M815/St.146.

44. Wood Transport.
c1910/13, pencil, 53.8 × 67.7cm.
Okk T1842/St.134.

45. Tree Felling.
c1912/13, charcoal, 26.9 × 40.2cm.
Okk T1820/St.131.

46. Lumberjack.
1913, oil/canvas, 130 × 105.5cm.
Okk M385/St.133.

47. Workers Digging around a
Tree.
1915(?), oil/canvas, 105 × 134cm.
Okk M431/St.15.

48. Man Digging.
1915(?), oil/canvas, 100 × 90cm.
Okk M581/St.150.

49. Harvesting Machine.
c1916, oil/canvas, 68 × 90cm.
Okk M296/St.149.

50. Haymaking.
c1916, oil/canvas, 131 × 151cm.
Okk M3867/St.139.

50. ▲

Workers Returning Home
1913–1920

51. Workers Returning Home.
1910/13, charcoal, 69.27 × 49cm.
Okk T1858/St.156.

52. Workers Returning Home.
c1913, brown crayon, 42.8 ×
26.3cm.
Okk T1849/St.158.

53. Workers Returning Home.
1913/15, oil/canvas, 201 × 227cm.
Okk M365/St.155.

54. Workers Returning Home
and a Man with a Top Hat.
1916, lithograph, 20.2 × 26cm.
Okk G/1506-7/St.167.

55. Workers on the Road.
After 1916, litho crayon, 48 ×
60cm.
Okk 2428/St.166.

56. Workers Returning Home
from Eureka.
After 1916, watercolour, coloured
crayons, charcoal, 57 × 77.9cm.
Okk T1854/St.160.

57. Grenadier-Strasse, Berlin.
1919/20, lithograph, 26 × 30cm.
Sch. 496/Okk G/11425-5.

58. Workers Returning Home
from Eureka.
1920, oil/canvas, 80 × 139cm.
National Gallery, Oslo.

Freia Project 1921

59. Workers Leaving the Factory.
1921, coloured crayons, 14 ×
44.8cm.
Okk T2025/St.168.

60. Mechanic Meets his
Daughter.
1921, coloured crayons, 15 ×
25cm.
Okk T2029/St.169.

61. Trinity Church.
1921, coloured crayons, 13 ×
27cm.
Okk T2030/St.170.

62. Trip to Grefsenåsen.
1921, coloured crayons, 15.1 ×
26.9cm.
Okk T2028/St.171.

63. In Studenterlunden.
1921, coloured crayons, 13.8 ×
27cm.
Okk T2027/St.172.

64. A Chat by the Fence.
1921, coloured crayons, 14.8 ×
30cm.
Okk 2026/St.173.

65. Couple on the Pier.
c1921, coloured crayons, 17.1 ×
25.2cm.
Okk T2018/St.174.

66. Workers and Horses in the
Street.
c1921, coloured crayon, 14.8 ×
30.5cm.
Okk T2041/St.175.

66. ▲

67. Workers Near Trinity Church.
1921, coloured crayon, 32 ×
14.6cm.
Okk T2019/St.176.

City Motifs, Building Work, Construction of the Studio 1920s

68. Galloping Horse in the Street.
1913 or later, coloured crayon,
20.7 × 26.7cm.
Okk T1848/St.177.

69. Children in the Street.
1913 or later, coloured crayon,
20.1 × 26.3cm.
Okk T440/St.178.

69. ▲

70. Workers in the Cellar.
1918 or earlier, oil/canvas, 90 ×
120cm.
Okk M155/St.187.

71. Horse and Cart in the Street.
c1920, watercolour, 49.1 × 61.2cm.
Okk T1841/St.179.

72. Horses in the Street.
Oil/canvas, 110 × 130cm.
Okk M426/St.181.

73. Street Workers.
c1920, etching, 15.4 × 17.3cm.
Willoch 197/Okk G/r182-3/St.185.

74. Street Workers.
1920, lithograph. 43.5 × 56.5cm.
Sch. 484/G/I418-30/St.186.

75. Fire.
1920/22, oil/canvas, 130 × 161cm.
Okk M824/St.194.

76. Worker Rolling a Barrel.
Watercolour, charcoal, 42.8 ×
60cm.
Okk T1838/St.189.

77. Worker.
1920s, black crayon, 11.3 × 14.5cm.
Okk T1788/St.190.

78. Worker.
1920s, black crayon, 11.3 × 14.5cm.
Okk T1789/St.191.

79. Worker.
1920s, black crayon, 11.3 × 14.5cm.
Okk T1790/St.192.

80. Worker.
1920s, black crayon, 11.3 × 14.5cm.
Okk T2346/St.193.

81. Workers Leaving the Building
Site.
c1920, oil/canvas, 127 × 102cm.
Okk M408/St.213.

85. ▲

90. ▲

82. Workers Leaving the Building Site.
c1920, charcoal, 50.3 × 37.3cm.
Okk T1791/St.214.

83. Men on the Building Site.
1920(?), oil/canvas, 68 × 90cm.
Okk M298/St.219.

84. Building Work.
c1920, oil/canvas, 95.5 × 99.5cm.
Okk M154/St.220.

85. Building Work.
c1920, oil/canvas, 100 × 95.5cm.
Okk M156/St.221.

86. Worker and Horse.
1920s, oil/canvas, 125 × 160cm.
Okk M73/St.197.

87. Building Work.
1920s, watercolour, coloured pencil, 39.5 × 30cm.
Okk T1835/St.199.

88. Building Work.
1920s, watercolour, coloured pencil, 30 × 39.4cm.
Okk T1830/St.200.

89. Building Work.
1920s, watercolour, coloured pencil, 30.1 × 49.6cm.
Okk T1833/St.201.

90. Building Work.
1920s, watercolour, coloured pencil, 30 × 39.5cm.
Okk T1829/St.202.

91. Building Work.
1920s, black crayon, 31.9 × 50.6cm.
Okk T1827/St.203.

92. Building Workers under the Roof.
1920s, oil/canvas, 120 × 100cm.
Okk M161/St.211.

93. Building Work.
1920s, charcoal, watercolour, 30 × 39.4cm.
Okk T1831.

94. ▲

94. Building Work.
1920s, watercolour, coloured
pencil, 30 × 39.4cm.
Okk T1832.

95. Building Work.
1929(?), charcoal, coloured
pencil, 50 × 64.8cm.
Okk T1847/St.206.

96. Building under Construction.
1929(?), charcoal, coloured
pencil, 64.8 × 50cm.
Okk T1843/St.207.

97. Building Work.
1929(?), coloured pencil, 64.8 ×
50cm.
Okk T1846/St.208.

97. ▲

98. Building Work.
1929(?), coloured pencil, 64.8 ×
50cm.
Okk T2427/St.209.

99. Building Work.
1929(?), oil/canvas, 129 × 105cm.
Okk M872/St.212.

100. Carpenters.
c1929, oil/canvas, 82 × 109.5cm.
Okk M157/St.218.

101. Building Work.
c1929, oil/canvas, 71 × 100cm.
Okk M585/St.222.

102. Building the Winter Studio
1929, oil/canvas, 153 × 230cm.
Okk M376/St.223.

103. Building the Winter Studio
1929, ink, 22 × 29cm.
Okk T1814/St.224.

104. Building the Winter Studio
1929, oil/canvas, 149 × 115cm.
Okk M870/St.225.

The Town Hall Project
1927–33

105. Horse on a Building Site.
1920s, charcoal, coloured
crayons, 31.9 × 50.6cm.
Okk T1827/St.203.

106. Town Hall under
Construction.
1929 or earlier, watercolour, 70 ×
100cm.
Okk M986/St.228.

107. Town Hall under
Construction.
1929(?), coloured pencil, 40.8 ×
25.5cm.
Okk T1825/St.226.

108. Building of the Town Hall.
c1929, charcoal on unprepared
canvas, 200 × 128.5cm.
Okk M931A.

109. Building of the Town Hall.
c1929, charcoal on unprepared
canvas, 190.2 × 125.7cm.
Okk M932A.

110. Building of the Town Hall.
c1929, charcoal on unprepared
canvas, 190.2 × 125.4cm.
Okk M930A.

111. Building of the Town Hall.
c1929, charcoal, coloured pencil,
40.8 × 25.3cm.
Okk T1822.

112. Building of the Town Hall.
c1929, charcoal, coloured pencil,
40.8 × 25.3cm.
Okk T1823.

113. Building of the Town Hall.
c1929, coloured pencil, 38.3 ×
50cm.
Okk T1836.

114. Workers in the Snow.
c1929, black crayon, 27.5 × 58cm.
Okk T2351/St.273.

115. Workers in the Snow.
c1930, oil/paper, 181 × 250cm.
Okk M1041/St.274.

116. Workers in the Snow.
c1930/35, oil/canvas, 340 ×
570cm.
Okk 977/St.275.

117. Building of The Town Hall
c1929, coloured crayon,
41 × 21.5cm.
Okk T 2875.

Tour Venues

Newcastle Polytechnic Gallery	8 October – 30 November 1984
Aberdeen Art Gallery	12 January – 2 February 1985
The Barbican, London	14 February – 31 March 1985
City Art Centre, Edinburgh	18 April – 18 May 1985
Ulster Museum, Belfast	30 May – 24 June 1985
Walker Art Gallery, Liverpool	4 July – 18 August 1985

Lenders to the Exhibition

Munch Museum, Oslo
National Gallery, Oslo

Polytechnic Gallery

Exhibition and Tour organised by
Mara-Helen Wood

© Mara-Helen Wood 1984
Polytechnic Gallery
Library Building
Sandyford Road
Newcastle upon Tyne
NE1 8ST

Designed by Stephen & Sue Bland
Typesetting and Artwork by FOLIO 90
Printed by the Hindson Print Group

(Front and Inside Covers)
Haymaking
c1916 (Cat. No. 50)